ALL YOU WAN
Acupr
Dai~y ~ife

Edited by
Dr Savitri Ramaiah

New Dawn

NEW DAWN
a division of Sterling Publishers (P) Ltd.
A-59, Okhla Industrial Area, Phase-II, New Delhi-110020
Tel : 6916209, 6916165, 6912677
Fax: 91-11-6331241
E-mail : ghai@nde.vsnl.net.in
www.sterlingpublishers.com

All You Wanted to Know About - Acupressure in Daily Life
© 2000, Sterling Publishers Private Limited
ISBN 81 207 2301 5
Reprint 2001, 2002

Published by Sterling Publishers Pvt. Ltd., New Delhi-110016
Lasertypeset by Vikas Compographics, New Delhi-110029.
Printed at VMR, New Delhi.

Information for this series, has been provided by *Health Update*, a monthly bulletin of the Society for Health Education and Learning Packages. The Update is intended to provide you with knowledge to adopt preventive measures and cooperate with the doctor during illness for better outcome of treatment.

Contributor

 ALLOPATHY
Ms Himpriya Gupta
(Consultant, Acupressure, VIMHANS, New Delhi)

Preface

All You Wanted to Know About is an easy-to-read reference series put together by *Health Update* and assisted by a team of medical experts who offer the latest perspectives on body health.

Each book in the series enhances your knowledge on a particular health issue. It makes you an active participant by giving multiple perspectives to choose from — allopathy, acupuncture, ayurveda, homoeopathy, nature cure and unani.

This book is intended as a home adviser but does not substitute a doctor.

The opinions are those of the contributors, and the publisher holds no responsibility.

Contents

Introduction

Acupressure is one of the oldest healing systems, and it has existed in India and the Orient for several centuries. For years this traditional drugless therapy was confined to few countries until the western countries, especially the United States of America showed interest in developing and adapting acupressure.

Shiatsu of Japan, Acupuncture of China, and hand and foot reflexology of the east, etc., are various forms of acupressure. All these techniques are based on stimulation of specific reflex points in the body in order to provide relief from pain or other ailments. Our bodies have remarkable self-healing energy forces which are used by natural and all other holistic sciences of healing such as nature cure, acupressure, acupuncture, etc.

The healing energies flow through the body in specific pathways called meridians. Each of these meridians have nerve centres and reflex points in various parts of the body. In acupuncture, needles are inserted into these nerve centres and reflex points, whereas in acupressure, the healer's fingers apply pressure. Most of the reflex points where pressure is applied are located on the foot, hand, back, face, and the ears.

What is acupressure?

Acupressure is the process by which normal energy flow in the meridians is restored. Any obstruction or blockage in the flow of energy in the body on these meridians results in ill- health.

Tiny crystal-build up on the nerve endings can also disrupt the proper flow of energy impulses.

This interruption in the energy flow causes pain at specific reflex points on the respective meridians.

When pressure is applied to these reflex points, they are stimulated and the blockage to energy flow is released. Relief follows the normalisation of the energy flow.

13

Every organ, and part of the body has a reflex point on the hands and feet.

A deviation in the normal functioning or a change in the structure of various organs of the body induces pain in their corresponding reflex points on the hands and feet.

Acupressure applied to the selected points in the feet and legs to cure ailments is called *foot reflexology*. Pressure therapy applied to the hands is called *hand reflexology*.

Some healers use reflex points on the ears, face, head and scalp for treatment. Most reflex points used in Shiatsu of Japan are located on the back, abdomen and limbs.

Acupressure can be used to diagnose various health problems. A reflex point, painful upon touch, may mean that the corresponding organ has an abnormal function or structure, or both.

This abnormality may reveal symptoms of a disease especially in its early stages.

By applying pressure to the painful reflex point, the normal functions and structures of the organs can be restored over a period of time.

What are the reflex points on the feet and palm?

Generally the location of reflex points corresponds to the location of the organ in the body.

The organs to the right have reflex points on the right hand and foot, and those to the left have reflex points on the other hand and foot.

Organs located on both sides (such as kidneys, eyes, ears, etc.) have reflex points on both feet and hands.

Acupressure theorists divide the body into ten equal vertical zones that run the length of the body from the top of the head to tips of the toes and fingers.

Figure 1. Vertical zones of the body

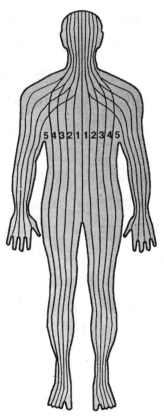

Thus, there are five zones on the right and five on the left side of the body as shown in Figure 1.

Each toe or finger on the feet and hands respectively is a part of a specific zone.

The palms and feet are divided into four horizontal parts to represent four parts of the body as shown in Figures 2a and 2b.

- Fingers, thumb and webs correspond to the head area.
- End of fingers and toes up to their middle correspond to the chest area.

Figure 2a. Horizontal zones of the body

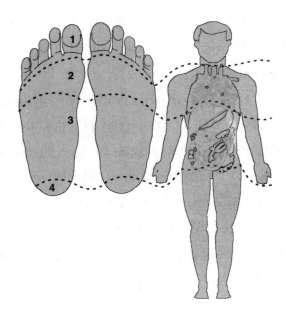

Figure 2b.

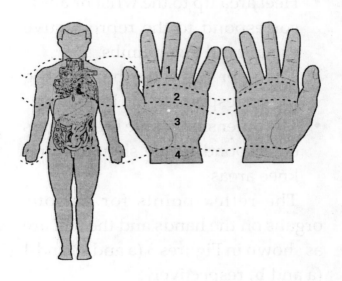

- Middle curved part of the foot and palm correspond to the abdomen and digestive organs and

- Heel area up to the wrist or ankle correspond to the reproductive organs and lower limbs.

- The outer side of the thumb or big toe correspond to the backbone.

- The outer sides of the little fingers correspond to the shoulder and knee areas.

The reflex points for various organs on the hands and the feet are as shown in Figures 3 (a and b) and 4 (a and b) respectively.

The reflex points of the face and their benefits are illustrated in Figure 5.

Figure 3a. Reflex points of major organs on the hands

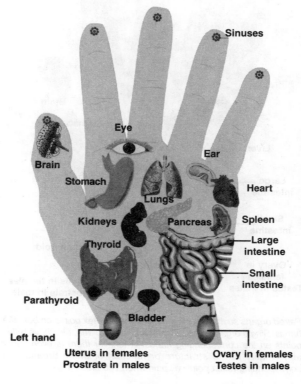

Sinuses

Eye

Ear

Brain

Heart

Stomach

Lungs

Kidneys

Pancreas

Spleen

Thyroid

Large intestine

Small intestine

Parathyroid

Bladder

Left hand

Uterus in females
Prostrate in males

Ovary in females
Testes in males

Figure 3b

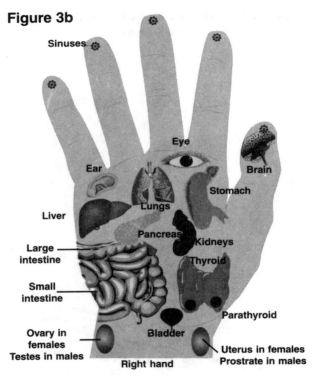

Sinuses

Eye

Ear

Brain

Stomach

Liver

Lungs

Pancreas

Kidneys

Large
intestine

Thyroid

Small
intestine

Parathyroid

Ovary in
females
Testes in males

Bladder

Uterus in females
Prostrate in males

Right hand

*Paired organs such as eyes, ears, etc., have reflex points on both the
hands. Single organs such as stomach, liver, spleen, etc., have reflex
points on the corresponding hands. Whenever there is even minor
abnormality in the structure or function of these organs, the
corresponding reflex point will pain when you press it.*

Figure 4a. Reflex points of major organs on the feet

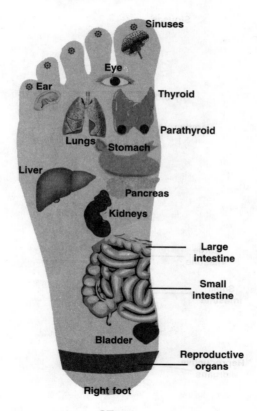

Sinuses

Eye

Ear

Thyroid

Parathyroid

Lungs

Stomach

Liver

Pancreas

Kidneys

Large intestine

Small intestine

Bladder

Reproductive organs

Right foot

Figure 4b

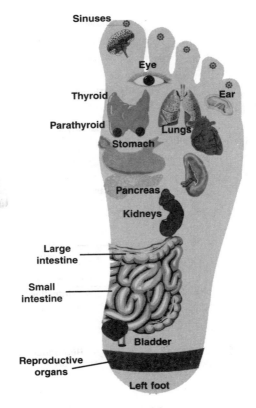

Sinuses

Eye

Thyroid

Ear

Parathyroid

Lungs

Stomach

Pancreas

Kidneys

Large
intestine

Small
intestine

Bladder

Reproductive
organs

Left foot

Figure 5. Reflex points on the face

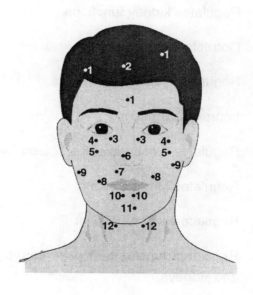

Benefits

- Increases mental energy.

- Regulating functions of vital organs and nerves.

- Regulates kidney functions.

- Corrects refractive errors.

- Regulates bowel movements.

- Improves digestion.

- Regulates functions of the spleen.

- Regulates lung functions.

- Regulates liver functions.

- Regulates functions of pancreas, bladder and kidneys.

- Relieves constipation.

- Regulates functions of genital organs.

What are the methods of applying pressure?

There are several ways of applying pressure in acupressure including reflexology.

The amount of pressure to be exerted will vary from person to person and in various parts of the body.

It is important that the reflex areas are held in a correct manner while applying pressure. If not, the desired effect may not be achieved.

The finger nails need to be trimmed before applying pressure in order to prevent them from pressing on the reflex points.

Rotating:

- The thumb should be rotated either clockwise or anti-clockwise on each reflex point, one after another.
- While rotating, the thumb is kept in contact with the reflex point so that a steady pressure is being exerted.
- The pressure points on the meridian are stimulated by an anti-clockwise movement and sedated by clockwise movement.

Pumping:
- This should be done by pressing the thumb pad on the reflex points.
- Pressure must be applied and released alternately.

35

Continuous movement:

- Called thumb walking or continuous movement of the fingers (called finger walking).
- The aim of this technique is to give a constant and steady pressure.
- In this technique, the thumb or the fingers "walk" along a specific pathway.
- They first press through the tip and then move to the next point by pressing through the flat of the first joint of the thumb or fingers.

- Finger walking can be done either with one, two or four fingers, depending upon the pressure points.
- Reflexes on the hands and back are normally treated by two-finger walking.

Rubbing:

- Rub the reflex points or area without any pressure.

Clutching:
- Clutching or squeezing should be done such as for the shoulder.

39

Vibrating:

- Where one palm is placed on another or one finger is kept on another and then manual vibrations are given.

Steady pressure:
- Pressure should be applied with the thumb or fingers such as on the back, thighs and back of the legs.

Twisting:

- Twist the limbs which are held in two hands.
- Move the muscle mass in clockwise and anti-clockwise direction.

Cupping:
- Here the skin and underlying muscles are held in the cup of the hand and a light pressure is given.

43

Your thumb or fingers may get tired very soon while applying pressure to various points in the body.

You can strengthen the thumb and fingers in three ways:

- Hold the two palms together in 'Namaste' pose and press the two hands against each other and hold for a count of ten. Release the pressure for a few seconds. Repeat the entire process for about ten times a day.

- Push the thumb away from the other four fingers that are held together. Join the fingers and thumb of the two hands. Press the finger tips including the thumb of the hands for a count of ten. Release pressure for a few seconds. Repeat the entire process ten times.

- Hold the fingers of the left hand with the right hand and push them backwards forcefully for a few seconds. Release pressure and repeat the process for ten times. Next, hold the fingers of the right hand with the left hand and repeat the above process.

What are the steps in treatment with foot reflexology?

The treatment process involves:
Relaxing the feet in four ways:

- massaging the top and sides of the feet and ankle,
- twisting the feet with both hands,
- rotating all the toes and ankle in both clockwise and anti-clockwise directions, and
- pulling and stretching all the fingers in one continuous and smooth movement.

Detailed techniques of relaxation are given in later sections of this book.

Massage of the upper part of the foot involves continuous pressure

49

through moving fingers in the five zones of the body. The direction of the moving fingers needs to be away from the heart, which means towards the toes.

- Pushing, pulling, rotating and twisting the big toe.
- Starting the pressure treatment from the left foot involves pressing the big toe. Follow by pressing all the other toes including their tips and webs.
- Stimulating reflex points of the thyroid and parathyroid glands. Stimulate the points for the neck.
- Stimulating reflex points for the chest area, windpipe, lungs and

thymus glands by applying pressure through a continuous and forward movement of the thumb.

- Stimulating organs of the abdomen including pancreas, adrenal glands, kidneys, bladder, spleen. Stimulate the stomach, small and large intestines, liver, gall bladder and appendix in the same way.
- Stimulating the ovary and uterus in females and prostrate glands in males.
- Applying pressure through a continuous movement of the thumb on the outer edges of the

foot along the big toe and little toe on reflex points of the backbone, shoulder and knee.

- Ending the treatment session by stimulating the reflex points of the kidneys.

It is desirable that you walk barefoot as it stimulates the reflexes on the feet and therefore stimulating the energy flow in the entire body.

There are some acupressure points that are forbidden during pregnancy. It is, therefore, advisable that pregnant women undergo acupressure sessions under the direct supervision of a trained specialist.

Similarly, people who have had recent surgery should also undergo acupressure sessions with a trained specialist only.

Acupressure should also be avoided by people who are seriously ill or are taking regular medicines for serious health problems such as cancer or diabetes.

Acupressure treatment should be stopped for some time if you have sweating of the hands.

Sweating indicates reaction of the reflex areas to the massage. When you resume acupressure, reduce the pressure while giving the massage.

In case there is sweating on the entire body and you begin to feel cold, the treatment needs to be stopped immediately.

In such cases, you need to be covered with a warm blanket and pressure applied on the reflex areas of the solar plexus, pituitary and the heart. Pressing these reflex areas will ensure quick recovery.

After completing the treatment session, you are likely to feel relaxed, and sometimes sleepy. You may feel the urge to pass urine more frequently and the urine may smell pungent.

If some of your long-lasting health problems had not been cured earlier, their symptoms may aggravate after the acupressure treatment. However, all these reactions are temporary and disappear after a few sessions.

There are some simple reflexology techniques that you can practise regularly for maintaining normal health. These include:

- Walking barefoot on rough or uneven ground for at least five minutes everyday.
- When the soles come in contact with the uneven ground, they stimulate almost all the organs of

the body. Walking on dew-drenched grass early in the morning for about five to ten minutes. This also helps stimulate reflex points of almost all organs.

- Hold the hands like a cup with fingers apart. Press the tips of all five fingers of one hand against the finger tips of the other hand. Hold the position for two to three minutes and repeat it once or twice a day. Pressure against the finger tips stimulates all vital organs of the body.

- Interlock the fingers and press them together for two to three minutes twice a day.

- Firmly clench your teeth continuously for two to three minutes twice a day.

What are the relaxation techniques?

People who are under stress need to relax and stimulate the flow of vital energy in the body before practising acupressure or reflexology.

Detailed below is the sequence of relaxation techniques, which are best done by another person.

- Hold the padded part of the foot just below the toes with both hands.
- Move them forward and backward very rapidly in order to stretch the muscles of the foot.
- Place one hand across the top of the foot and clench the other hand into a fist.

- Place the fist on the opposite side of the foot.
- Rotate the foot clockwise and anti-clockwise.
- Place the fingers on top of the foot in such a way that the thumb supports the sole.
- Move the fingers in small circular movements on the top and sides of the foot and the ankle.
- Massage with small and gentle strokes the top and sides of the foot.
- Start from the ankle and move up towards the toes.

- Place the thumb in the reflex point of the solar plexus and the fingers on the top of the foot.
- Take a deep breath and hold it while pressing on the reflex point.
- Release the breath as the pressure is released slowly.
- The above steps then need to be repeated on the other foot.
- You can repeat the entire process with the hands too for enhanced benefits.

How does acupressure affect the body?

Acupressure helps the body to achieve an equilibrium in its functioning by:

- Increasing the blood supply.
- Regulating the blood flow to the ailing part.
- Clearing the blocked energy flow along the meridians.
- Restoring the disrupted nerve impulses to normal.
- Improving muscle tone.
- Restoring chemical or hormonal balance in the body.
- Relieving mental and physical stresses in the body, thereby increasing energy levels.

The benefits of acupressure can be observed over a period of time. The duration of treatment will depend upon the severity of the disease and/or health problem.

What are the advantages of acupressure?

Acupressure is an effective, preventive and curative method for a large number of health problems and diseases.

It is safe, simple and easy to learn and practice, and is suitable for people of all age groups.

The advantages of acupressure are as follows:

- It is a non-invasive and non-addictive system.
- It does not aggravate any symptoms.
- Occasionally the symptoms may aggravate for a few days, especially if the health problem is long-lasting.

- It has no side-effects or with-drawal symptoms.
- It can be used to diagnose several health problems in the initial stages itself without any laboratory tests.
- It can be used along with all other systems of medicine.
- It improves overall health and focuses on the entire body rather than the affected part alone.

What are the health problems for which acupressure is recommended?

Diseases for which acupressure is reported to be effective include:

- allergies and asthma
- disorders of the backbone
- spondylosis
- arthritis and other diseases of the bones and joints
- paralysis
- disorders of the muscles
- hormonal disorders
- bronchitis
- cold and sinusitis
- migraine
- stress-related nervous disorders
- heart conditions

- high blood pressure
- disorders of the liver and digestive system
- irritable bowel syndrome
- ulcerative colitis
- kidney diseases
- sleeplessness, headache
- obesity
- menopause
- diabetes
- general weakness including anaemia and a general feeling of being unwell.

Acupressure points and their application for a few common health problems are listed in the following pages and illustrated in Figures 6 - 10.

You may need to continue the medicines prescribed by your doctor even while taking acupressure treatment.

Acupressure can only reduce the severity of symptoms and hasten recovery.

Application of acupressure points for common disease or health problems

Head and forehead

1 Light pressure, clockwise rotation on top of the head and six points around it for 20 seconds/30 counts.

Benefits

Relieves headaches, sleeplessness, constipation, fatigue, weakness and increases memory.

2 Rotation with moderate pressure along the hairline for five counts on each point, 3 rounds.

Benefits

Helps manage mental disorders, loss of hair, sleeplessness and headache.

3 Steady pressure on the "bindi" point in the middle of the forehead with two middle fingers for 20 seconds each, 3 times.

Benefits

Bring peace, relieves sinusitis and headache, relaxes the eyes and increases mental energy.

4 Steady pressure or rotation on two points roughly above the centre of

each eyebrow for 20 seconds or 30 counts.

Benefits

Relieves headaches, fatigue, relaxes the eyes and controls sinusitis.

5 Steady light pressure on the sides of the head, roughly at the level of the eyes for 30 seconds.

Benefits

Relieves headache and symptoms of sinusitis.

6 Place thumb on the depression at the back of the head and move the

head backwards. Hold this position while applying steady light pressure. Press for 30 seconds, once. Repeat thrice.

Benefits

Relieves headache, sleeplessness, mental stress, pain due to spondylosis and helps control high blood pressure.

7 Press the two points on the bone on each side of the depression at the back of the head once for 30 seconds on both the sides.

Benefits

Relieves headache, sleeplessness, mental stress, spondylosis, cold, stiff neck, dizziness and helps control high blood pressure.

8   Press three points in a straight line between the depression in the back of the head and crown once for 20 seconds on each point.

Benefits
Relieves headaches and helps control low blood pressure.

9   Light pressure on the skull points located in five lines with fingers in a manner that cover the entire skull. 10 points on the side lines above the ears, 12 points on next

lines and 14 points on the mid line
of the skull. Repeat twice.

Benefits

Relieves headache, symptoms of
sinusitis, releases tension and
prevents loss of hair.

Face

1   Pinch the eyebrows by placing the
    thumb under the eyebrow with
    moderate pressure, three times.

Benefits

Reduces mental tension, relaxes
the eyes and reduces symptoms of
sinusitis.

2 Press the inner edge of the eyebrow upwards and apply steady pressure for 30 seconds. Repeat three times.

Benefits

Increases concentration and improves thinking capacity.

3 Light pressure on one point on either side of the eyes and three points above and below them for twenty seconds each. Repeat three times.

Benefits

Relaxes the eyes.

4   Light pressure on the back of the
    ears.

Benefits

Regulates blood pressure and
reduces ear and face pain.

5   Massage the ear: The shape of the
    ear is like the shape of the unborn
    child in the mother's womb, with
    the head pointing down. The
    curve of the ear is like the
    backbone. Press each point for 20
    seconds. Repeat thrice.

Benefits

Covers maximum reflex points of
the spine and brain and therefore
helps regulate their functions.

6   Points on the nose: (a) press top of the nose inwards on both sides with index finger and rotate it ten times, release pressure, (b) press middle of the nose upwards under the bone with index finger, move head downwards and rotate the finger ten times and release pressure, (c) press edge of the nose inwards with index fingers, rotate the figure tip ten times and release pressure. Stimulate the three points thrice, one after another.

Benefits

Relieves symptoms of sinusitis, allergies and any other disorders of the nose.

7 Press three fingers under the cheekbone, rotate them three times and release pressure. Repeat three times.

Benefits

Relieves symptoms of sinusitis, reduces cough, and improves digestion.

8 Steady deep pressure on the tip of the nose for 30 seconds and release pressure. Repeat thrice.

Benefits

Improves digestion.

9 Steady pressure for ten counts on point under the nose and above the upper lip. Repeat three times.

Benefits

Brings relief as first aid during seizures, fainting and unconsciousness.

10 Press the four jaw points along the edge of the jaw from ear to the chin on both sides for 20 seconds on each point.

Benefits

Corrects locked jaw and reduces pain in the jaws.

11 Steady pressure with index finger under the centre of the chin or holding the chin with thumb supporting it below the chin for one minute. Release pressure. Repeat thrice.

Benefits

Provides relief from constipation.

Neck

This is done at the nape of the neck in three steps: (a) steady moderate pressure with the finger along the edge of the back of the neck till the shoulders, (b) press the point where the neck and shoulders meet with the thumb and (c) squeeze the shoulders with fingers and then release pressure. Repeat thrice.

Benefits

Relieves headache, pain in the neck region and helps you feel more energetic.

Chest

1 Press lightly the end of the neck between the collar bones, bend the neck forward and hold in this position for a count of ten. Repeat thrice.

Benefits

   Helps control asthma, cough, cold
   and difficulty in breathing.

2 Light pressure with fingers on
   specific points on four lines on
   each side of the chest for 3
   seconds. Release pressure for 1
   second. Repeat thrice on each
   point.

Benefits

   Helps control asthma, cough.

Abdomen

1 Nine points on the abdomen as indicated in Figure 4.

Benefits

Corrects constipation and other digestive disorders.

2 Light pressure on the three points shown in Figure 5 for a count of ten on each point. First point is located three fingers below the navel and the other two near the prominent part of the hip bone. Repeat thrice.

Benefits

Regulates menstruation and relieves symptoms of menopause.

Hands

1 Pressure with moving fingers on the shoulder, squeezing or pinching the shoulder muscles.

Benefits

Reduces headache and pain due to cervical spondylosis, frozen shoulder.

2 Steady thumb pressure for three seconds each along the four lines dividing the arms in a way that cover eight arm points. Release pressure. Repeat three times on each point.

Benefits

Frozen shoulder, pain in the arms.

3 Press three points on the elbow:
   on the centre and two sides.
Benefits
   Corrects tennis elbow and relieves
   constipation.

4 Press three points on the wrist.
Benefits
   Reduces pain in the wrist and
   stiffness in the fingers.

5 Rotating pressure for ten rounds
   with fingers at the back of the
   palm along the five fingers.
   Repeat thrice.
Benefits
   Reduces pain in the wrist and
   finger joints.

Figure 6a. Reflex points for general bodyache and increasing general strength

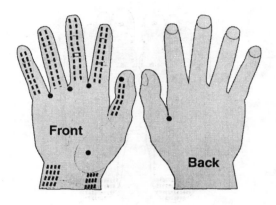

For tiredness of the body due to excessive work or a sense of being unwell, reflex areas of adrenal

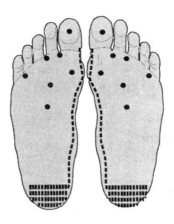

glands, diaphragm (the membrane that separates the chest from the abdomen) and the entire spine need

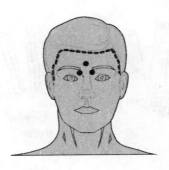

to be stimulated. In addition, two points each on the urinary bladder and kidney meridians and one point on the gall bladder meridian need to be stimulated.

Figure 7a. Reflex points for common cold and sinusitis

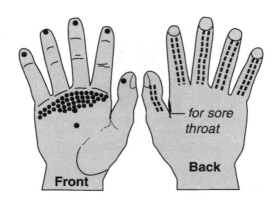

Treatment of sinusitis involves stimulation of reflex of the head, sinuses, upper lymph nodes, adrenal

Figure 7b.

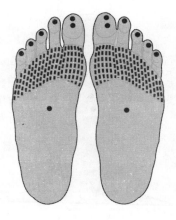

glands, neck and upper part of the
spine. Acupressure points include
two points each of large intestine and
spleen meridians and one each of gall

99

Figure 7c.

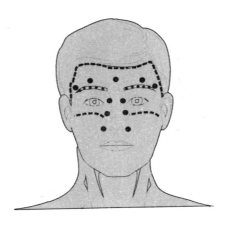

bladder and small intestine
meridians. All the points on the face
need to be stimulated thrice, for 20
seconds each, twice a day.

Figure 8a. Reflex points for headache and migraine

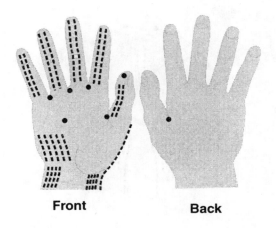

Front   **Back**

For treatment of headache and migraine, reflex areas of the neck, spine, all endocrine glands, intestines, eyes, ears, and the entire

Figure 8b.

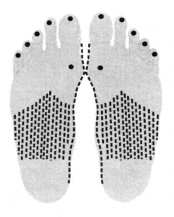

length of the fingers, thumb and the web in between needs to be stimulated. The point on the back of the hand is on the triangle of the flesh

Figure 8c.

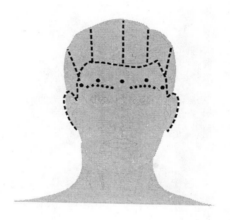

between the thumb and index finger.
At this point, push the thumb
downward and inwards for 15 to 30

Figure 8d.

seconds or give intermittent pressure.
This point should not be pressed for
a pregnant lady.

Figure 9a. Reflex points for stress-related nervous disorders

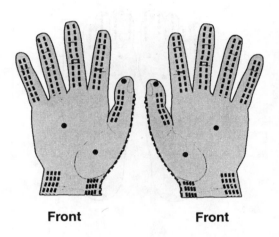

Front   Front

Stress can lead to a large number of symptoms and health problems. One of the simple ways to control any problems with the mind or brain is

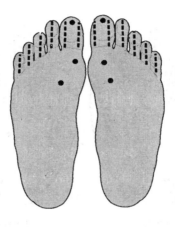

to give deep, intermittent pressure on the reflex area of the brain, on the thumbs and big toes for two minutes each, twice a day. While acupressure

Figure 9c.

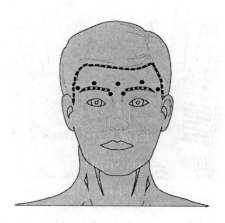

can reduce stress-related mental disorders, it is important to practise other relaxation techniques such as yoga, meditation, etc., for more effective management of stress.

107

Figure10a. Reflex points for disorders of the digestive system

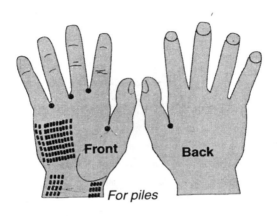

For problems related to the stomach (such as indigestion, burning in the stomach, ulcers, increased acidity, etc.), you need to stimulate the stomach area on the foot or hands by continuous movement of the thumb.

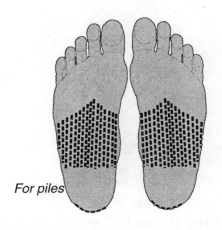

For piles

Cover the entire area by taking small
steps with the thumb. Whenever you
feel pain at a particular point, give
deep and intermittent pressure with
the tip of the thumb at that point.

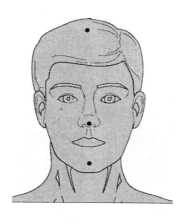

Repeat three times before moving to other parts of the stomach area. You can also pinch the web between the big toe and second toe or thumb and index finger for one to two minutes twice or thrice a day.

In case you have problems related to the intestines (such as constipation, increased gas in the bowels, diarrhoea, colitis, etc.), you need to give pressure through continuous movement of the thumb in the reflex area of the intestines. Just as for the stomach area, give intermittent deep pressure at all the points where you feel pain. Stimulate the reflex points of the intestines twice a day. You also need to stimulate points indicated in Figure 11.

Figure11. Reflex points on the abdomen

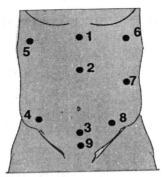

1. Upper part of the stomach
2. Small intestine
3. Bladder
4. Cecum (blind-ended pouch at the junction of small and large intestines), valve at the junction of small and large intestines and appendix
5. Liver
6. Spleen
7. Descending colon
8. Sigmoid colon
9. Rectum

Method of application:

- Apply the pressure in a sequential manner, starting from point 1 and ending at point 9.
- Apply pressure for a count of 5 (3 seconds) at each point with both palms, with left palm on top of the right.
- Inhale deeply before applying pressure and gradually increase pressure to give a deep penetrating effect.
- Exhale as you release the pressure.
- Repeat the above steps once or twice.
- Repeat the process with finger tips of the index, middle and ring fingers of both the hands joined together. Repeat thrice.

Figure12a. Reflex points for knee joint pain and arthritis

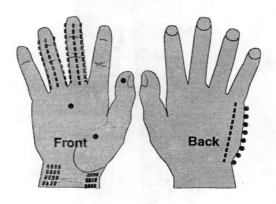

For arthritis, reflex areas of the spine, hip and knee need to be stimulated. Specifically for knee pain because of arthritis, you need to press with your

thumb the four points on the front of the knee, two of which are roughly 4-5 inches above the knee cap and two below the knee cap. Press for

Figure12c.

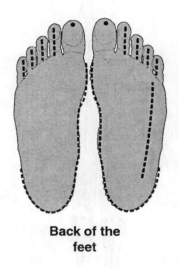

Back of the feet

three seconds and then release pressure. Repeat the process thrice. At the back of the knee, you need to

Figure12d.

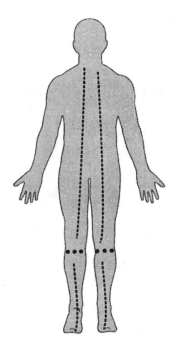

press three points with the thumb for
three seconds each. Repeat thrice.

Figure13a. Reflex zones on the ankle and sides of the feet

1. Knee
2. Hip joint
3. Fallopian tube
4. Ovary/testis
5. Abdominal wall
6. Pelvic area

7. Elbow
8. Upper arm
9. Ribs
10. Shoulder joint
11. Head
12. Gall bladder

Thigh and pelvic area

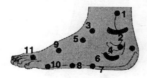

Left outer side   **Right outer side**

Figure13b.

1. Fallopian tube
2. Thigh and pelvic area
3. Uterus, prostrate, testes
4. Anus
5. Sacrum (bones of the backbone in the pelvis)
6. Bladder
7. Abdominal wall
8. Backbones at and below the waist area
9. Backbones in the chest area
10. Ribs, muscles of the chest
11. Backbone in the neck area
12. Head

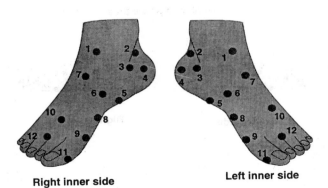

Right inner side   **Left inner side**

118

What are the specific guidelines for practising acupressure?

To begin with you need to learn the correct method of stimulating the reflex points on the hands and feet and acupressure points in various parts of the body from a trained and an experienced practitioner of acupressure.

- Normally each reflex point on the hands and/or feet is stimulated for about three to five seconds and released for two to three seconds before applying pressure again at the same point.
- You can repeat this process three times for each point twice a day.

- To prevent diseases of the endocrine glands and to maintain normal health, you need to stimulate the reflex points of all the endocrine glands on both the hands.
- This should be done for about five to ten minutes everyday.
- For treatment of various ailments, the reflex points of the affected organs need to be stimulated for one to two minutes each.
- In addition, reflex points of other important organs such as the kidneys, digestive system, lymph,

etc., need to be stimulated for three to five seconds each.

- The type of pressure used for stimulation of these points will depend upon the organs involved.
- The heart point should be stimulated only by a trained and experienced acupressure specialist.
- Acupressure treatment should be avoided half an hour before or after meals, or bath.
- The pressure should be applied in a manner you can tolerate. Excessive pressure can be harmful.

- Avoid using hard or sharp objects to exert pressure close to bones to prevent nerve injury.
- When stimulating the reflex points provide support on the other end with your hand.
- End the acupressure session by stimulating reflex points for the kidneys and adrenal glands.

What is the
therapeutic value of
jewellery?

Indians have been practising acupressure through customary rituals, festivals and yoga in their day-to-day lives.

Some say jewellery was worn around the body to seek the same effect.

Ancient Indian texts describe the following twelve types of jewels for women, some of which have a clear therapeutic value.

Tikka:

- This is the jewellery worn from the top of the head to the forehead.
- It presses the points on the urinary bladder meridian and the pineal gland.
- Pineal gland is a pea-sized mass of tissue attached to the brain at the back of the skull.
- Wearing a *tikka* helps regulate activities of the brain and gives peace of mind.

Shish phool:

- This is worn on the forehead and presses on the points on the urinary bladder meridian.
- Wearing *shish phool* helps control headache and sleeplessness.

Nose ring:

- This is the jewel worn on the nose.
- It reduces the risk of infections of the nose, and makes the sense of smell stronger.
- The nose ring is also connected to the heart meridian.

Earrings:

- Earrings worn on the lower part of the ear helps to regulate the activities of the brain and improve memory.
- They also help to reduce the risk of infections of the tonsils.
- Silver earrings can reduce or control excessive hunger.
- Earrings worn on the upper part of the ear can prevent hernia.

Armlet:

- This is worn on the arms, between the elbow and the shoulder.
- Armlets press the points on the lung and heart meridians.
- They strengthen the heart muscles.

Bangles and kadas:

- These are worn on the wrist, and they press the reflex points of the ovaries and uterus located on the wrist.

- They, therefore, help regulate the functions of the reproductive organs.

- The sounds produced by the bangles can help control mental disorders.

Rings:

- A ring worn on the fourth finger of the left hand presses the reflex points of the heart.
- This is perhaps why married women were advised to wear rings on this finger.
- Rings worn on other fingers press reflex points of the brain, eyes and ears.

Necklace:

- A necklace that extends from the neck to the chest presses shiatsu points of the heart and lungs
- This in turn, helps regulate their functions of these organs.

Choker:

- This is a tight necklace that rests on the neck only.
- It presses shiatsu points of the thyroid and parathyroid glands.
- It helps to regulate their functions.

Kamarbandh:

- This is the jewellery worn around the waist.
- It presses the local points of the ovaries, uterus and kidneys and points on the spleen meridian.
- *Kamarbandh* helps control menstrual disorders and improves digestion.

Anklets:

- These are worn on the ankles.
- They press reflex points of the ovaries and uterus just like bangles and *kadas* do.

Toe rings:

- These rings press on the reflex points of the eye, ear and nerve centres.
- Toe rings also help correct imbalances of the *solar plexus*, regulate ovulation and reduce labour pains during delivery.
- Copper or silver rings on the big toe helps in controlling high blood pressure and brain disorders.
- Solar plexus is the network of nerves high in the back of the abdomen.
- It is important to remember that the pressure applied by wearing

jewellery is not strong, it's only a continuous light pressure which helps to regulate the functions of various organs, especially the reproductive organs and the brain.

What is the role of acupressure instruments?

A wide range of acupressure instruments are available in the market for exerting pressure and thereby treating diseases.

Most of these instruments are made of wood, plastic and rubber. It is advisable that you buy and use acupressure instruments only after consulting a specialist.

Detailed below are some of the instruments used for acupressure:

Jimmy:

- This is a long instrument with a large number of small pyramid-shaped elevations.
- It is made of either plastic, wood, rubber or metal.
- Jimmy is used for pressure on hands and feet reflexes.
- It should not be used near a bony area as it may injure the nearby nerves.
- The pressure exerted by jimmy should be moderate and not heavy.

Cervical jimmy or mini roll:

- This too has a large number of small pyramid-shaped elevations.
- In addition, it has a handle connected on the two sides.
- You can roll the cervical jimmy on the area to be stimulated.
- It is normally recommended for exerting pressure on tender and delicate parts of the body.
- You can use it on neck and along the sides of the fingers, three times on each site.

Foot roller:

- This is a long rod-like instrument with a large number of small pyramid-shaped elevations.
- Foot roller is normally recommended for pressing general reflex points of the feet.
- You need to sit on a chair and keep one foot at a time on the roller and move it backwards and forwards for three minutes.
- Repeat the same process on the other foot.
- Foot roller tones up the body, increases blood circulation and therefore makes you feel more energetic.

Hand roller:

- It is similar to the foot roller but smaller in size and is recommended for stimulating reflex points on the hand.
- You need to press and roll the instrument between the palms for two to three minutes. Hand roller relieves tension, general body-ache and fatigue.

Spine roller with magnet:

- This roller is made of four magnetic wheels for use on the backbone.
- The wheels press the two sides of the backbone and therefore stimulate the spinal reflex points.
- You need to apply slow and bearable pressure with the spine roller and move it from the neck to the hip in both directions.
- You can also extend the roller application up to the legs.
- Spine roller is normally recommended for cervical spondylosis, backache and sciatica.

Power mat:

- This is also called a pyramid pad and contains small pyramid-shaped elevations and a curved middle part on which the sole rests.

- Walking on the power mat for three to five minutes can help manage acidity, diabetes and backache, relieve tension, reduce weight and increase energy.

- It is also effective for headache, migraine, sinusitis, asthma, sleeplessness and loss of memory.

- Best results are obtained if you use the power mat twice a day, early in the morning and before going to bed.

- In case the skin of your feet is very delicate, you can cover the power mat with a thin cloth before use.

- It is important to remember that there are several types of power mats and you need to consult a specialist for the most effective type.

Multiplex massager:

- This instrument has four rows of rollers attached to a handle.
- It is very effective for relieving mental and physical fatigue by releasing blockages to the flow of vital energy of the body.
- It can be used to apply pressure on every part of the body.
- It is normally recommended for headache, mental tension, sleeplessness, backache and pain in the shoulders.

HEALTH UPDATE

YOUR PERSONAL MEDICAL ADVISOR

SOLUTIONS FOR ANY MEDICAL PROBLEM, AT YOUR FINGERTIPS

HEALTH UPDATE gives you detailed information on common diseases and ailments from five different perspectives- **Allopathy, Ayurveda, Nature Cure, Homoeopathy** and **Unani** in a concise and easy to understand format, complete with graphic descriptions, general information, health tips and much more.

SUBSCRIPTION

India ☐ 1 year-Rs. 300/- ☐ 2 years-Rs. 500/- ☐ 3 years-Rs. 750/-

International ☐ 1 year-$25 ☐ 2 years-$45 ☐ 3 years-$60

☐ Yes, I would like to subscribe to **Health Update**, the monthly health bulletin

Name: Mr./Ms...
Address (mention nearest landmark)..
....
City:.................... State:.................... Country:....................
Pin:.................. Tel:.................. Fax:..............email:....................
Age/Profession...

☐ I am sending by Cheque/DD No..................................drawn on
(specify bank).. for Rs...................
dated.......................... favouring **HEALTH UPDATE**.

☐ Please charge my American Express Credit Card

Credit Card No. ☐☐☐☐☐☐☐☐☐☐☐☐☐☐☐☐☐☐☐☐☐☐☐☐☐

Card Expiry Date..................Card Holder's Signature...........................

Date of Birth...........................Tel. (O) .... (R)..................

Direct this subscription form to:
HEALTH UPDATE, D-31, Defence Colony, New Delhi-110024, India.
Tel.: 4622863. Fax: 91-011-4698150. email: savitri_ramaiah@vsnl.com

152